The Third Incarnation:
The Eternal Value System
Part 3

By Bob Mumford

LIFECHANGERS ®

P.O. Box 3709 ❖ Cookeville, TN 38502
931.520.3730 ❖ lc@lifechangers.org

PLUMBLINE

Published by:

LIFECHANGERS ®
LIBRARY SERIES

P.O. Box 3709 | Cookeville, TN 38502
(800) 521-5676 | www.lifechangers.org

All Rights Reserved
ISBN 978-1-940054-22-3

The Third Incarnation:
The Eternal Value System
Part 3

By Bob Mumford

Personal Note

As I have been putting this series together, I have felt, at times, as if I would explode. Sometimes the clarity of what I see in God's purposes for His people and the Kingdom is blinding; at other times I feel like true clarity is still out of focus. As I approach the autumn of my years in searching out mysteries of the Kingdom it seems my journey might be compared to a huge jigsaw puzzle. Early in my life I laid out the borders (By the way, I am piecing this together without the picture on the box!). I have been completing some of the more obvious sections through the years. Some pieces I have tried to force where they did not fit. Others I have simply had no idea where they belonged in the larger picture of Father's grand panorama of redemption.

I have not taken this journey alone. My faithful wife, Judith, has been an unending source of support, valuable input, and often a needed reality check! Other fellow travelers on the moving pathway have contributed immeasurably to my understanding. Most of all, they have helped me to have the confidence and courage to continue the quest. I feel as though I am not chasing anything, but the burden is truly chasing me.

Please understand that what I present here is still a work in progress. If everything does not yet seem to be complete, that is because it isn't. However, be assured that the full picture of God's purposes is still emerging and in time: "We shall know fully just as we also have also been fully known" (I Corinthians 13:12).

Preface: Review

The Third Incarnation is the final book in a series of three Plumblines entitled *The Eternal Value System.* If you have read the first two, *Engaging the World* and *Follow Me*, then this review of those two editions will help reset the focus and flow of the message. If, however, you have not read the first two, this will serve to introduce you briefly to the foundation of this present edition. The first two editions are available through Lifechangers.[1]

We are Simply Unable to Govern Ourselves

Human history bears out the sad reality that the human race is not capable of ultimately governing itself. Over five millennia of recorded human history indicates that in spite of our amazing advances in knowledge and technology, the same fundamental evils of the fallen human mind continue to make

---

1 Order through Lifechangers© by Bob Mumford: www. lifechangers.org

life difficult or perilous. Our value systems govern our judgments, choices, and priorities. On the most basic level everything and everyone is governed by one of two internal, spiritual value systems. These value systems are not merely codes of behavior but are spiritual forces that permeate everything.

The most pervasive value system in modern culture is the eros[2] value system. This force empowers these seven foundational motivations identified as the Seven Giants:

1. Look good

2. Feel good

3. Be right

4. Stay in control

5. Hidden agenda

6. Personal advantage

7. Remain undisturbed

---

2 The essential meaning of eros is the desire or intention to possess, acquire, or control. Eros does not seek to be accepted by its object, but to gain possession of it. Eros has an appetite or yearning desire that is aroused by the attractive qualities of its object. Eros, in Greek philosophy, came to mean that which is loved for the purpose of personal satisfaction. Anders Nygren, *Agape and Eros*. Philadelphia, PA: Westminster Press, viii-xvi.

The bottom line is to please myself at any time and for any reason. Once eros becomes the dominate value system of any human institution, it becomes subject to corruption, decline, and death in varying and increasing forms.

However, through the Basilea [kingdom] of God's eternal spiritual government, we are given hope for a fractured and hurting world. God's Basilea is expressed in God's eternal value system. This is not merely a standard of ethical behavior. It is the very governmental expression of His Agape nature—God is Agape.

Agape is the MO (mode of operation) by which God relates to and governs the entire cosmos and all of human kind. Here are four expressions of His Agape:

1. I will keep My word

2. I will not encroach on that which is another's[3]

3. I will look for an opportunity to do you good

4. If I cannot do you good, I want you to know My intent is not to do you harm

In His faithfulness He keeps his word, first, about Himself, who He is and how He desires to be known. This is demonstrated by the fact that He is

3 I have barrowed the first two of these from Richard Maybury. *The 17-Word Solution.* ©2016, Ethics Solutions

a covenant keeping God. He binds Himself to us in His person, in the Word which is Christ, and without this assurance all else in meaningless.

Even though Creator God has the right, as the absolute Sovereign of creation, He will not usually encroach on human sovereignty even when we decide against Him. He holds us humanly responsible to choose how our lives are to be governed. He extends the offer of His Kingdom, but He does not mandate that we accept it.

God is looking for opportunities to do us good. Because God is good, He can only do good. However, beyond that, God is not capriciously good—He is aggressively good.

God wants us to understand that it is never His intent to harm us. How contrary this is to the picture painted by religion in general that God is angry and waiting, fire and lightening kindled and ready, to meet out vengeance on the world for offending Him. Jesus seeks to correct this perverted understanding.

The Gospel carries in it the message of hope to a hurting world. However, the "gospel" is too often marketed as, "Accept Jesus, your sins will be forgiven. He'll make everything right, and you get to go to heaven when you die." I believe, the Gospel Jesus presents is something like: "God has a government, why don't you try it!"

It is a government expressed in His eternal value system. This government is not a set of Kingdom rules. We cannot DO the eternal value system, but we must BECOME the eternal value system. Jesus did not just teach the Eternal Value System, He was the incarnational demonstration of it. We are not capable of making this incarnational transformation in and of ourselves. The Father has issued an invitation for us to follow Jesus and become transformed into His image by means of what we called the moving pathway.

The Moving Pathway

The Moving Pathway is Father working through all things, conforming us to the image of His Son and reconciling us to Himself. Simply stated, our destination has already been determined by God, Himself!

> And we know that God causes all things to work together for good to those who love God, to those who are called according to His purpose. For those whom He foreknew, He also predestined to become conformed to the image of His Son, so that He would be the firstborn among many brethren.[4]

Being conformed to the image of Christ engages Father's intentionality for us. Like Jesus, we are to become incarnational manifestations of the eternal value system. Jesus explained to His disciples that they were to love their enemies and bless those who

4 Romans 8:28-29.

cursed them. We are to be present in the world as light and salt affecting, changing, influencing, and giving life to those we encounter.

Jesus set the mark far higher than any of us can hope to reach. To live authentically requires transformation of our very persons. The only pathway to authentic transformation is through a living, dynamic relationship with Jesus. The moving pathway is a relationship not a rulebook. I cannot emphasize this too strongly. We will reach the goal of the pathway if we will follow the One who victoriously embraced the pathway Himself.

The Transformation of Our Image

As we allow Jesus to mentor us on the pathway, we will become more human as God intended. Jesus was not only a revelation of the Father; He was also a revelation of what a human person was created to be. If God created Adam and Eve to be humanity in its fullness and pronounced it "very good," then Jesus was also humanity in its fullness as the Last Adam.[5] At the core of becoming truly human is a complete and comprehensive change of our identity. The human identity tied to our fallen state, will now be transferred to being sons and daughters of the Kingdom.[6]

Restoring Our Responsibility

Human responsibility is in desperate need of

5 1 Corinthians 15:45
6 Colossians 1:13

restoration. The absolute foundation of restored human responsibility is choice. Simply stated, choice constitutes our human responsibility on the moving pathway. As we encounter "all things" we are presented with forced choices. We will encounter situations, people, and circumstances where we have no option but to make a choice.

Each time we choose to embrace the eternal value system there are three foundational choices that are required if we are to fully follow through.

First, we must choose to hear His voice and engage the wisdom of spiritual discernment. If we are not sure of the way, we have a Guide, the Holy Spirit. It is wise to listen to what He has to say.

Second, we choose to engage a life of repentance. Religious tradition has often focused repentance on sin and/or sins. However, in the New Testament it is most generally used in connection with a change of mindset or values, resulting in a change of lifestyle. If we refuse or are unable to leave the religious, fallen mindset that continually focuses on personal failures and best efforts, we will never be able to live in freedom, poised joyfully toward the Father.

Third, we must choose to become comfortable with mystery. The Moving Pathway is a mystery and part of a larger eternal mystery—the Mystery of Christ Himself. The Cosmic Christ is the Mystery of all creation, "in whom are hidden all the treasures of wisdom and knowledge."

Failure to embrace and become comfortable

with the mysterious conundrums of the moving pathway is one of the major reasons people stumble (offended, scandalized). We can fall away from the faith or choose to live our lives with underlying anger or resentment toward God that overrides our intimacy, joy, and peace. To be comfortable with Mystery is to be comfortable with God being Himself without our permission or understanding! It is letting go of the need to know and control.

Choice—it is ours minute by minute, day by day, year by year. It is the glorious freedom and privilege God has given us to choose life – that we might live!

THE THIRD INCARNATION

GIVING THE WORLD ITS FATHER BACK

The governmental functioning of the Kingdom of God is expressed in the eternal value system. The role that God takes in His governmental relationship to His people is expressed by many different pictures and metaphors, but I believe the role which most accurately expresses His true nature and heart is that of a Father. Creation is designed to be governed by a Father! The first patterning of "government" in a child's life comes from her or his father.

Our daughter, Beth, as a licensed Christian counselor, is continually confronted with deep and difficult wounds and failures in the lives of those whom she is called to assist. It has been her experience that a very high percentage of the problems people struggle with can be traced back to issues in their relationships with their fathers. Where there has been a dysfunction, absentee, or abusive father there can be deep-seeded issues with rejection, insecurity, lack of identity, and the inability to function relationally. My experience in years of counseling has been similar, as other professionals, both Christian and secular, will testify.

We have, by created design, the innate need to be "fathered" into life. God's government is based on fathers and families. When God called Abraham He declared His blessing on Abraham's seed would go to all the families of the earth. Paul, in writing to the Ephesians said, "I bow my knees before the Father, from whom every family in heaven and on earth derives its name."[7] "Family" is a particular Greek word that points back to a progenitor or ancestor. Each of these, Paul infers, is in some manner fathered by God.

When mankind rejects the fatherhood of God, they instinctively look for an earthly substitute. Israel asked for an earthly king, "like all the nations." They wanted a king to judge them, lead them, and fight their battles[8], which God had been doing since they had been delivered from Egypt hundreds of years before. They wanted a father—one they could see! At the end of the Old Testament we hear God lamenting, "If I am a father, where is my honor?"[9] But God's final word to Israel before four hundred years of silence was a promise to restore heartfelt fatherhood and sonship, lest the land be smitten with a curse.[10]

Four hundred years later God speaks again not in the voice of a prophet, but "in a Son."[11] This Son's very person demonstrated, by what He taught and did, that God desired to be known as a Father above all else. Throughout human history mankind has followed Israel's pattern in looking for fatherhood in a human leader: a chief, a king, an emper-

7 Ephesians 3:14-15
8 See 1 Samuel 8:20
9 Malachi 1:6
10 Malachi 4:5-6
11 Hebrews 1:3

or, a president, a pastor, a philosopher, a guru, or a cult leader. Something deep inside of us wants to be told what is right and wrong; provided with strong leadership; and ensured of our security. However, as was witnessed in the kings of Israel, the leadership has failed to one degree or another being subject to the corruption of the fallen mindset. In short, the world needs its real Father back.

Purpose of the Kingdom

Here is a simple but penetrating question that the Lord challenged me with recently: "Does the Kingdom of God transform society or is its purpose to populate heaven?" As followers of Christ, and therefore recipients of the great commission, the answer to this question should radically affect how we live our lives.

Since the beginning of the twentieth century the emphasis of evangelism has been focused more on "saving souls" (individuals) for heaven than on saving the world as a human society. There is an indisputable mandate to introduce people to the Lord through the new birth, but the new birth is the invitation and equipping to enter the Kingdom and not an end in itself.

Please note the context of the new birth in John 3 is the Kingdom of God and not going to heaven. I am sure this off-center focus is due at least in part to the dual emphasis in America on end time prophecy (hang on for the rapture and let Jesus sort out the mess after the tribulation); and the focus on church growth as the measure of gospel success. Neither of these have done much to transform the contemporary culture of the West, which in turn has permeated most of the rest of the world.

I would suggest that the focus of the Great Commission is getting the Kingdom of God into the world. And the goal of the Kingdom in the world is not to populate heaven but to restore the Fatherhood of God to all creation.

Three Incarnations

The word incarnation is never used in the New Testament, but it is broadly used to describe a non-material entity (being, spirit, idea) becoming embodied in some material form. Specifically in Christian theology it is used of the eternal Son taking on human flesh and form: "[whom] we have heard, [whom] we have seen with our eyes, [whom] we have looked at and touched with our hands, concerning the Word of Life."[12]

This may beg the question: why would the infinite, eternal God, Who is Spirit, choose to express Himself in any limited material form? To answer this we must restate a fundamental concept we have emphasized throughout the previous Plumblines in this series. God is in His very essence a relational being. Witness the reality—He is relationship living within the Sweet Society of the Trinity. Out of this circle of Agape and friendship He desires to

12 1 John 1:1. Also see Philippians 2:6-8.

manifest His glory; reveal His person, to know and to be known through incarnation.

First Incarnation

God first chose to incarnate His nature in the creation of the material universe. He did not incarnate His person, but He created this physical universe to reveal "His invisible attributes, His eternal power, and divine nature."[13] Judeo-Christian revelation has understood this from its very roots. David declared:

> The heavens are telling of the glory of God;
> And their expanse is declaring the work of His hands.
> Day to day pours forth speech,
> And night to night reveals knowledge.
> There is no speech, nor are there words;
> Their voice is not heard.
> Their line has gone out through all the earth,
> And their utterances to the end of the world.[14]

Creation is a primary vehicle of God revealing Himself and His nature.[15] The Apostle John in his

13 Romans 1:20
14 Psalms 19:1-4
15 We must carefully distinguish this understanding of creation as an expression of God's nature from pantheism, which states that God and creation are one. While all things are "in Christ" (Col. 1:16-17) God, the person of the Creator, is separate from and transcendent to all creation.

gospel declares Christ the Creator as "The Word," (Greek word Logos). Logos is used in Scripture to refer to an expression of thought or something close to "God's Idea." It is not the mere name of an object. It is the embodying of a concept or idea.[16] When John declares, "all things came into being through Him [the Logos], and apart from Him [the Logos] nothing came into being that has come into being,"[17] he is saying that creation is the expression of God's thoughts, His ideas. The logos expresses the pattern after which all things were made. Paul echoes this idea when he refers to Christ as "the firstborn of all creation."[18] All creation bears some measure of His image.

Experts in art can recognize if a painting is created by Rembrandt, Dali, or Picasso by the style of expression each uses. Something unique of the creator is revealed in his or her creation. In like manner, as we look at the physical universe it reveals to us something of the nature of God and the spiritual universe. For example, death and resurrection is an almost universal process from stars to plants to people. It pictures the eternal, inviolable, spiritual truth that for new life to be born some form of death will proceed it.

16 Vine's Expository Dictionary of Biblical Words, Copyright © 1985, Thomas Nelson Publishers.
17 John 1:3
18 Colossians 1:15.

Corruption and Entropy

Another universal spiritual truth mirrored in the physical universe is what the Scripture refers to as corruption. Corruption is the tendency for everything and everyone to spiral downward into chaos and death. After the fall of man all creation was subjected to corruption.[19] Jesus seemed to sum up the process when He spoke about treasures on earth where "moth and rust destroy [Gk. corrupt, disfigure] and thieves break through and steal." [20] Here corruption is in the biological world (moth), the material world (rust), and in society (thieves). Corruption is ubiquitous and irreversible in the natural once it is initiated.

It is not my purpose to expand the concept of corruption[21] but rather to use it as a point of comparison to a law from the world of physics called entropy. Without becoming overly technical we will say for our purposes that entropy is the degeneration and increasing disorganization of energy within a closed system. A closed system is one that is not subject to any outside input or influence. For example, consider your own home on a very cold winter's day. It is kept warm by your furnace or an electrical heating system because it

19 Romans 8:19-20
20 Matthew 6:19
21 I unpack the concept of corruption extensively in a Plumbline, "Breaking the Power of Corruption" available from https://lifechangers.org for purchase or as a free download.

is an open system. That is, the electricity from the local power company is coming into your home (system) from the outside to provide heat or to run the furnace. However, if something interrupts the flow of electricity, e.g. an ice storm breaks power lines, your home will immediately become a closed system. As soon as heat can no longer be generated inside your home the heat will begin to dissipate and the home will begin to cool until it is the same temperature as the air outside. This is the process of entropy working in regard to the heat in your home.

Open and Closed Systems

Open and closed systems operate in the spiritual universe. At creation man (Heb. Adam) was an open system spiritually. The life and presence of God energized his spirit and his being continually. When sin entered through disobedience, in some mysterious manner the life flow of the Spirit of God was damaged in mankind. "In the day you eat of it [fruit of the tree of knowledge] dying you shall die."[22] Adam and Eve did not drop dead when they disobeyed God, but they became closed in some manner to the life of God. The process of entropy, or biblically, corruption, was initiated and would ultimately result in their physical deaths.

Contrary to what much of religion teaches, God did not close the system--we did! Please consider

---

22 Literal Hebrew rendition of Genesis 2:17, see Young's Literal Translation or Concordant Version of the OT

carefully Paul's words to the Romans:

> For the wrath of God is revealed from heaven against all ungodliness and unrighteousness of men who suppress the truth in unrighteousness, because that which is known about God is evident within them; for God made it evident to them. For since the creation of the world His invisible attributes, His eternal power and divine nature, have been clearly seen, being understood through what has been made, so that they are without excuse. For even though they knew God, they did not honor Him as God or give thanks, but they became futile in their speculations, and their foolish heart was darkened. [23] [Italics mine]

God's revelation of Himself was clear through the first incarnation, the creation that was open to the human system. However, humanity with sufficient understanding made the decision to close their system (hearts and minds) off to the knowledge of God.

Notice that God's wrath[24] is not expressed in some sort of fiery judgement on humankind.

---

23 Romans 1:18-21

24 Greek *orge* does not indicate judicial condemnation, rather a strong negative emotion or passion: a brief, intense, expression of emotion, from which we gain the word orgasm.

Instead, God honors the second point in the eternal value system by not encroaching on man's decision to close the door on Him. In essence God said, "You think you know best? Fine. I'll let you do it your way!" Humankind had closed its "system" to the knowledge of God. The inevitable process of corruption (entropy) began a downward slide ending in social disintegration and anarchy.

The millennia of human history bears tragic witness to the disintegration and collapse of empires, cultures, and civilizations. For some only scraps and pieces in archeological digs remain to remember their former glory. Many died through internal moral and political decay or the abuse of creation's resources. Others grew weak and were conquered by military or cultural conquest. The process of decay merely runs its inexorable course.

Father's Open System

God is a loving creator. He never closes Himself from His creation. He continues to bless and provide in a most generous and gracious manner. Consider how God continues to function according to the second value of the eternal value system—I will look for an opportunity to do you good!

- Sun and rain (Matthew 5:45)
- Life, breath, and all things (Acts 17:25).
- The blessing of Abraham (Genesis 12:3)

- The revelation of His person through the incarnation of Christ (John 1:9, 14, 18; Hebrews 1:2-3)

- The cancellation of sin through the work of Christ (2 Corinthians 5:19; 1 John 2:2)

As we gaze back through redemptive history, we see God continually injecting Himself into our world. We see His intended purpose of halting the inevitable corruption to reconcile His creation to Himself.

God initiated His active penetration into our closed system when His glory appeared to Abraham. He called him out of worshiping other gods and purposed to give him an inheritance in the purposes of God. Abraham was introduced to the moving pathway through which he obtained the promise of a physical heir and became the father of all who believe. God's purpose, promise, and oath was that in him "all the families of the earth would be blessed."[25]

Abraham's seed became the physical nation of Israel commissioned to manifest to the all nations the knowledge and wisdom of Jehovah. Even though Israel failed to embrace the challenges of their journey on the moving pathway, God continued to move undeterred in His intended purpose to open the human system to Himself—a personal incarnation in the person of Jesus the Christ.

25 Genesis 12:3

Second Incarnation

It is reflective of the Father's very nature that He did not send His Son into the human system as a conquering champion to inaugurate the arrival of the Messianic Age foreseen by the prophets. Indeed, that would have been the Son of David whom the nation of Israel was expecting and for whom they longed. But rather than forcing His Kingdom on the world and establishing His government with a rod of iron, He came inauspiciously. He came as a human servant, emptying Himself of glory and power to present an offer to participate in His coming government through the new birth. Who could have expected the Eternal One to step into His creation manifesting the second eternal value—I will not encroach on that which is another's.

We cannot seem to find a way to govern ourselves that is free of the corruption (entropy). Corruption seems to be inherent in all human systems of government because they operate from the base of the eros-driven, fallen mindset. Christ's nature was to be the nature for His Kingdom.

Imperial Systems

Unfortunately, "Kingdom" has historically been understood as imperial in nature. Imperial comes from a Latin root meaning "to command" or "set in order." The key to understanding a created human kingdom is by nature it is self-referential and self-preserving. Rome, to secure its borders and to expand its power, conquered and controlled one nation after another until its empire expanded over most of Europe and Mediterranean world. This type of kingdom is characterized by a centralized, hierarchal government. It most often seeks to expand its power either through external conquest (however benign or benevolent in appearance) or through increased internal control of those who are within its realm—requiring conformity to a culture or creed that supports the imperial system.

Remember these words:

- Centralized, hierarchal
- Conquest
- Control
- Conformity
- Corruption

They are the nature of imperial government. Imperial goverment will almost inevitably expand, become self-preserving, and take on a life of its own.[26] Communism was (and is) a classical imperial system; reread the words above and it becomes glaring. The centralized power may be a king, a dictator, an emperor, a chief, a president, a political party, an oligarchy, a religion, or a cultural or political philosophy. The form of the system is not as important as the value system it embodies.

---

26 For an in depth study of this phenomenon, consider ordering *Dr. Frankenstein and World Systems*, available through lifechangers.org, or Amazon.

Has Christianity ever been imperial? Of course it has. Please witness the Crusades, the Inquisitions, the religious wars that raged in Europe all in the name of establishing "pure Christianity." Under the banner of advancing Christian civilization, colonial empires cruelly subjugated or destroyed indigenous peoples all over the world.

Is it possible for denominations, doctrinal systems, spiritual movements, and individual churches to become empires? In the early seventies I was personally involved in what came to be known as the Discipleship Movement or Shepherding Movement. It grew out of a genuine need to give pastoral care and direction to multitudes of individuals who had been touched by the Charismatic Outpouring and had left or been asked to leave traditional, denominational churches. What began with the best motives and intentions quickly became imperial, transgressing the second eternal value.[27] It encroached deeply into the lives of individuals, families, and congregations under the threat of "missing the Kingdom" or being "disfellowshipped". This well intended beginning imposed deep wounding on many, wonderful people.

The Kenotic Kingdom

Jesus never intended His Kingdom to be imperial! He patterned, taught, and commissioned

---

27 I will not encroach on that which is another's.

a kenotic Kingdom. Kenosis is the Greek word that describes Jesus' personal journey of humility from the throne to the cross. Here is the progression:

- Christ Jesus, who, although He existed in the form of God, did not regard equality with God a thing to be grasped,
- but emptied Himself,
- taking the form of a bond-servant,
- and being made in the likeness of men.
- Being found in appearance as a man,
- He humbled Himself by becoming obedient to the point of death,
- even death on a cross.[28]

Even though the Messiah was prophetically identified as the Suffering Servant in Isaiah, the religious leaders of Israel could not receive Him. They had become thoroughly imperial in their mindset and were looking for the son of the warrior king David to restore Israel to its former glory. They did not have room for a kenotic peasant who preached love for their enemies! This mentality was so deeply engrained that the disciples asked Jesus just before His ascension, "Now are you going to restore the Kingdom [of David and Solomon] to Israel?"

Consider Jesus' own testimony of Himself:[29]

---

28 Philippians 2:5-8
29 Matthew 20:28; Luke 22:27; John 6:38; John 5:30; John 10:15; Luke 22:19: Matthew 26:28; Luke 22:42

"The Son of Man did not come to be served, but to serve and give His life.."
"I am among you as one who serves . . ."
"I came not to do my own will . . ."
"I came to do the will of Him who sent me."
"I do nothing of my own initiative . . ."
"I lay down my life for the sheep . . ."
 "This is my body given for you."
"My blood . . . poured out for many."
"Not my will but yours . . ."

Jesus modeled kenotic leadership throughout His life. He healed, delivered, taught, and fed multitudes to the point of exhaustion. He raised the dead for the grieving, provided wine for an embarrassed host, and befriended prostitutes, political traitors, low-life's, the uneducated, the irreligious, and the outcasts of society. He ultimately begged forgiveness for those who rejected and crucified Him. He continually reversed the power of corruption by imparting the life that resided in Him. He endured the dullness of the disciples and their jockeying for position, ultimately washing their feet and finally fixing them breakfast on the beach. In all, Jesus lived a kenotic life based on the eternal value system—motivated by eternal, uncreated Agape! He was penetrating the closed system of the fallen mindset giving the world its Father back.

He enjoined those he taught to live a kenotic life style. If someone wants your shirt, give him your coat as well. Go a second mile. Love those who hate you as enemies. Bless those who curse you. Pray for those who persecute you. Do good expecting nothing in return. Have mercy. If someone takes from you, do not demand it back. Do not take the front seat at dinner. Do not practice your religion to be noticed.

With His disciples he pressed the point even further. If you want to become great, become a slave of all. The first shall be last and the last first. Wash one another's feet like I washed yours.

Living the Eternal Value System

In Jesus' prayer to His Father on His last night with His disciples He made this amazing statement, "I have manifested Your name to the men whom You gave Me out of the world."[30] What was the name He made known to the disciples? Elohim, El-Shaddai, Yahweh, Jehovah, Adonai? These names had been well known to the Jewish people since the time of Moses. What was the name Jesus manifested? Allow me to answer with an excerpt from a booklet by my good friend and fellow laborer in the Kingdom, Derek Prince, who went to be with the Lord in 2003.

> What was the name which Jesus manifested to His disciples? When you read the "high priestly prayer" you will find the name. What is it? It is "Father."

30   John 17:6

This name occurs six times in John 17. Jesus came to manifest the name of the Father. The word manifest is important, because He didn't just come to talk about the name "Father." He came to demonstrate it.

Secondly, how did Jesus demonstrate the reality of the Father to His disciples? By living like a Son of God. Jesus was never frightened, never perplexed, never in despair. He never failed to know what to do. Why? Because the Father was always with Him.

The disciples saw in the way Jesus lived a totally different kind of life. They were familiar with the prophets. They were familiar with Moses. They were familiar with men who had done tremendous signs and wonders and spoken mighty words. But here was a Man who lived knowing that He had a Father in heaven.

Jesus, by His whole life from beginning to end, manifested the name "Father." That is why He came. That is why God sent Him—because only a Son could reveal the Father. The prophets could speak about God and teach about God, but they could not reveal Him. Nor could they manifest Him. Only the Son could reveal the Father.[31]

Jesus gave the world its Father back! A true father is the embodiment of kenosis, motivated by Agape and pouring forth himself through the eternal value system toward his family even to the giving of his life. If all fathers lived in this character the world would be transformed in one generation.

God had raised Israel to be a son, manifesting His glory and Fatherhood to the nations according to the promise of Abraham. However, lamenting through the prophet Isaiah, the Father seems to exclaim in utter frustration, "Sons I have reared and brought up, but they have revolted against Me!"[32] God's final word to Israel before 430 years of silence was a promise to restore lost fatherhood. He would turn the hearts of the fathers back to the children and the children to the fathers halting the progressive corruption. God's fulfillment was personally showing up in a Son. His Father heart turns in mercy and compassion.

The Third Incarnation

As the Father revealed Himself in the first born Son, He now desires in like manner to reveal Himself in a multitude of sons and daughters living

---

31 Derek Prince, Father God; © 2015 by Derek Prince Ministries – International
32 Isaiah 1:2

out the kenotic Kingdom—a third incarnation. The followers of Jesus lived out a kenotic Kingdom for two centuries following Pentecost and turned the world upside down. However, with the official recognition of Christianity under the Emperor Constantine in the fourth century the Church gradually became imperial and progressively lost her unique salt, light, and yeast.

Church history has known many great world-shaking ambassadors for Christ who changed nations and cultures by their kenotic witness. Patrick of Ireland, Francis of Assisi, and Mother Theresa immediately come to mind. How different church history might have been if these had been the norm.

Jesus was approached by a lawyer who asked what he should do to inherit the life of the coming Kingdom. Jesus asked him how the Law read to him. He answered, "Love God and love you neighbor."

"Right," answered Jesus. "Do that and you will have life."

Being a typical lawyer he wanted to make sure he was on the right side of the Law. He asked, "And who is my neighbor?"

Jesus went to the heart of the matter with a parable, the Good Samaritan. The priest and the Levite avoided an inconvenient situation. But a Samaritan:

- "felt compassion"—identified with the man's suffering

- "came near"—did not avoid an unpleasant situation
- "bound his wounds"—got his hands dirty
- "put him on his own beast"— walked himself
- "brought him to an inn"—saw to his immediate needs (out of his own pocket)
- And looked to the man's future

The lawyer would have known that in other circumstances the Jew would have held the Samaritan, who had been beaten, in utter contempt, probably cursed him and even spit on him. "Go and live like that," Jesus told the lawyer. In other words, if you want to live (Zoe life, God's Life), live a kenotic lifestyle. Jesus removed the idea of "neighbor" from being my little clique who believes and lives within my comfort zone. The world is my neighbor! The racist who hates me, the terrorist who would kill me, the businessman who cheats me, the abusive alcoholic, the unfaithful mate, the homeless addict, the person who spreads false gossip about me—they are all my neighbors. I am called to love them even as I love myself. We love just as the Father loves, not at a distance, abstractly, but up close and personal, identifying with their condition.

Likewise, a wealthy young man asked Jesus what he must do to inherit life. Mark records that "Jesus felt love for him." His desire was intense as witnessed by his sincere devotion to the Law.

"What do I still lack?" He asked.

"One thing," replied Jesus, "You are full of yourself, go sell all you have and follow me in a life of kenosis."[33]

I fervently trust you are seeing a vision for Father's sovereign design for the third incarnation. Great programs and campaigns will never transform the world if they are rooted in some imperial vision that only wants to expand the church and get people "saved." Only the incarnational reality of the Agape motivated, kenotically empowered application of the eternal value system can disrupt and unseat the principalities and rulers (the five arche's [34]). Those who are willing to be led into this Agape life will reign in the power of Christ's resurrection.

Perhaps we may understand anew Paul's cry:

> But whatever things were gain to me, those things I have counted as loss for the sake of Christ. More than that, I count all things to be loss in view of the surpassing value of knowing Christ Jesus my Lord, for whom I have suffered the loss of all things, and count them but rubbish so that I may gain Christ . . . that I may know Him and the power of His resurrection and the fellowship of His sufferings, being

---

33 See Mark 10:17-27
34 Five ruling spiritual powers, or empires, 1) Family, 2) Culture (ethnicity), (3) Religion, (4) Politics, (5) Economics

conformed to His death; in order that I may attain to the resurrection from the dead.[35]

The power of Christ's resurrection alone can reverse the power of entropy in the earth. Wherever Jesus went He reversed the seemingly inexorable power of corruption by healing, delivering, enlightening, forgiving, accepting, demonstrating— "doing good and healing all who were oppressed by the devil, for God was with Him.[36]" The light of Agape and the power of the resurrection alone can penetrate the closed system of this present age.

Creation is to be delivered by the manifestation of the mature children of God through the third incarnation.[37] How then are we to give ourselves with responsible intent to the Father's ultimate purpose in redemption—the restoration of His Fatherhood and the reconciliation of all creation to Himself?

I do not believe there is a special formula or a series of steps which, if we will follow them, can genuinely transform us into the image of the Son. To be an incarnate ambassador offering the Father to the world is a journey that must be desired and willingly embraced.

Allow me to offer five disciplines, perhaps I should say mindsets, which if we will give ourselves

35 Philippians 3:7, 8, 10.
36 Acts 10:38
37 Romans 8:19

to them will allow the Father to be manifested to a hurting world.

Five Mindsets

1. Abide! Jesus knew how to abide in His Father and out of His abiding to manifest the Father's being. Jesus told us that apart from Him we can do nothing. That's pretty drastic! But it makes perfect sense if we can embrace the fact that the Kingdom is a relationship and not a transactional set of principles. His resurrection life flowing through a dynamic relationship is the means by which He manifests His true purposes through us and the means by which we navigate the moving pathway.

Abiding is His most urgent command. Hundreds of excellent books have been written on the subject and countless sermons preached. Yet, I find that the "how to" remains nebulous in the minds of many earnest disciples. Please allow me to make two observations which may prove helpful.

First, abiding focuses on the eternal now. Much of our daily attention is focused on the future, often yielding fear, anxiety, and worry; or on the past bringing up regret, guilt, and blame. God revealed Himself as, "I AM"—the Eternal Now. His Name is not "I was" or "I will be." In some mysterious manner being aware and being present in the now ties us into the eternal, uncreated reality of God. The past and future are His. The past is buried in the waters of baptism. The future is governed by His predestined purpose. Our responsibility is the choices of the now.

Second, true abiding is a function of our human spirit more than our minds and emotions. "Abide in Me and I in you."[38] Not only are we to abide it Him, He abides in us—in our human spirit. An empowered human spirit will take ascendency in our persons in order to maintain us in a presence of faith, rest, and peace.[39] We must not seek so much to fill our minds with more knowledge and go to more conferences. We must find our personal "abiding place" in our spirits.

2. Live out of the eternal value system. Endeavoring to live and relate out of these four simple values in daily situations and relationships is a practical manner of "presenting our bodies as living sacrifices." We discover, to our surprise, that we are transformed and our minds are renewed with a revolutionary understanding of the Kingdom of God. This may be the thrust of the progression Paul presents to us in Romans 12:1-2.

- I will keep my word

- I will not encroach on that which is another's

- I will look for an opportunity to do you good

---

38 John 15:4
39 I would challenge you to read Appendix II where I have given what I believe to be the correct emphasis on the human spirit in Romans 8:3-10 and Galatians 5:16-23.

- If I cannot do you good, I want you to know my intent is not to do you harm

3. Embrace kenosis. As we endeavor to live out of the eternal values, the opportunities to be or to become kenotic will be abundant! Kenosis is one of the most mature forms of Agape, the Absolute of the Universe. A useful measure of the maturity of kenotic Agape is 1 Corinthians 13. Each of the factors of Agape are aspects of Christ's own character. The reason that "Agape does not fail or disappear" is due to the fact that God has given us Himself. God is Agape.

4. Choose to stay on the Moving Pathway. James tells us to rejoice in the moving pathway because we will develop endurance (meaning to abide under). Simply choosing to abide in Father's itinerary will lead to maturity and wholeness lacking in nothing.

5. Stay focused on the finish line. Father's goal is for us to become mature sons and daughters who are able to say, "If you have seen me, you have seen the Father."[40] If that sounds grandiose or sacrilegious, then we have not fully grasped the intent of the third incarnation. Our goal is not to become divine. Our goal is to become fully human as God intended—like Jesus.

Where We Started

In the first volume of this series of Plumblines, our journey began with a group of leaders seeing

40 John 14:9

problems with no answers. We have proposed that they are seeking the government of a Father who would lead us in love as a family. That family would express itself in the eternal value system. Envision with me for a moment a world ruled by these values:

I will be true to my word.

- No broken treaties
- No broken contracts
- No forsaken marriage vows
- No unfulfilled promises
- The end of inflated promises, spin, and propaganda
- No more "posing," hypocrisy, saying one thing while meaning another

I will not encroach on that which is another's.

- Wars would cease
- Terrorism would end
- Slavery and human trafficking would stop
- Theft and personal violence would be no more
- Exploitation of peoples, individuals, and the environment eliminated
- Adultery would no longer ruin marriages
- Personal boundaries would not be violated physically, emotionally, verbally, or sexually

I will look for an opportunity to do you good.

- The poor of the world would be remembered (swords beaten into plowshares, spears into pruning hooks[41])

- The world would have each other's backs.

- Society's excessive inequality socially and economically would flatten out

If I cannot do you good, I want you to know my intent is not to do you harm!

- Security among nations

- Freedom from social fear

If this sounds unreasonably idealist and utterly unattainable, please be reminded that this is the picture of the fulfillment of the new earth foreseen by the prophets of Israel concerning the messianic age. I believe it is also the "age to come" foreseen by Jesus and the writers of the New Testament. Likewise, many cultures, religions, and even modern fiction look forward to a similar utopian age. There is a universal longing set in the hearts of all mankind "that they would seek God, if perhaps they might grope for Him and find Him."[42] Anything less would leave the new creation and the Father's purpose in reconciling all things to Himself through Christ short of completion.

---

41 Isiah 2:4
42 Acts 17:27

Some object that this can only take place when Jesus comes personally to set things in order. Indeed, He will come again. But before He returns, Creation must experience the revealing of the mature sons and daughters of the Kingdom to free all creation from its slavery to corruption. In other words, before Jesus comes for His saints, He will come in His saints. He will fulfill not only the first and second incarnation, but radically so in what we have identified as the third incarnation.

Finale

Hopefully, we are now prepared to consider what may be described as an authentic "Kingdom look at the future" and how the concept of sonship will define and determine how that future will conclude. It is breath-taking in its simplistic clarity and purpose: "Then comes the end[43] (Greek: telios, speaking of God's purpose being fulfilled). I have put these sequential facts in pure biblical order, with minimum human intervention. They are taken from 1 Corinthians 15:20-28, Amplified Translation:

20. "But the fact is that Christ (the Messiah) has been raised from the dead, and He became the first fruits of those who have fallen asleep [in death]." At the moment of Christ's resurrection all humanity, past, present, and future, was radically forgiven. Christ's obedience in time

---

43 I Corinthians 15:24

accomplished that which occurred "before the foundation of the world.".[44]

21. "For since [it was] through a man that death [came into the world, it is] also through a Man that the resurrection of the dead [has come]." The First Adam caused all humanity to die, to lose their Father as source of Life (Zoe). The Last Adam, who is Christ, reverses such entropy in order for humanity to be returned to its Creator. This was accomplished in Christ's resurrection.

22. "For just as in Adam all people die, so also shall all in Christ be made alive." Carefully stated, because of Christ's perfect obedience "All in Adam died; All in Christ (as Last Adam) shall all be made alive." This occurred "before the foundation of the world." It does not depend upon human response. It is a Sovereign declaration of the God who seeks to regain His human family! Radical forgiveness that does not depend on Human response.

23. "But each in his own rank and turn Christ (the Messiah) [is] the first fruits, then those who are Christ's [own will be resurrected] at His coming." Those who engage and receive Christ's Kingdom offer, "Follow Me, I will

---

44 Ephesians 1:4

make you,"[45] are Christ's first-fruits or Christ's own. "The Lord knows those who are His."[46]

24. "After that comes the end (the completion), when He delivers over the Kingdom to God the Father after rendering inoperative and abolishing every [other] rule and every authority and power." The "end" is dependent upon the breaking, annulling, or transformation of all principalities, false authorities, and power structures. This is due to the maturity and authority of "God's sons" as stated in Romans 8:19-21. Mature Sons are the source of freedom from corruption for all of creation! The Body of Christ is the hope of all creation. Sonship becomes destiny and purpose. Reception of Father's Kingdom offer made in the Person of Christ becomes "Christ in you (plural) as THE hope of Glory."[47] Father's purpose in the earth and the consequent, inexorable fulfillment of Abraham's Promise allows us to see why the Kingdom is required to be taken and given until Christ has rendered inoperative all opposition in alternate principalities, arches, and power structures.

---

45 Matthew 4:19
46 2 Timothy 2:19
47 Colossians 1:27

25. "For [Christ] must be King and reign until He has put all [His] enemies under His feet."

26. "The last enemy to be subdued and abolished is death." "Of the increase of His Kingdom there shall be no end,"[48] until He has put all enemies under His Feet. When He does, the last enemy, death, will be abolished.

27. "For He [the Father] has put all things in subjection under His [Christ's] feet. But when it says, All things are put in subjection [under Him], it is evident that He [Himself] is excepted Who does the subjecting of all things to Him." This information has strongly influenced my understanding of how and why radical forgiveness and the Kingdom offer are distinct in their appeal to hurting humanity. Christ completes His assignment, and with Him, we complete our assignment. We are co-heirs and effective participants in the completion of God's Choice of allowing frail humanity to represent Him to those who are seeking to know their Father—to know intimacy and uncreated reality.

28. "However, when everything is subjected to Him, then the Son Himself will also subject Himself to [the Father] Who put all things

48 Isiah 9:2

under Him, so that God may be all in all [be everything to everyone, supreme, the indwelling and controlling factor of life]." We now return to the original, rather hidden, theme of our thesis: What is man that you should give him so much attention? Why would God remove Israel's Kingdom authority? What are the issues that we may be missing? Sonship is not based on "doctrinal purity," but on affection: "It is yet to be seen, what God has prepared for those who love (Agape) Him."[49] Agape moves us to friendship with Christ. It gives opportunity for Christ to affirm something we all need urgently: we have a Father that cares! He is willing to resist and discipline. He seeks our very best.

"And this is eternal life, that they know you the only true God, and Jesus whom you sent."[50] To the very best of my biblical understanding, this verse summarizes Abraham's Promise that was originally given as God the Father's personal oath: in you, Abraham, all of the families of the earth shall be blessed! This oath cannot be aborted.

The primary and essential theme of the entire Bible is: God's faithful undertaking to restore His Own Fatherhood. We could carefully summarize this hidden theme in the New Testament to sound something like this:

49 I Corinthians 2:9
50 John 17:3

This Father, who loves the world, is determined to restore His Own Fatherhood to hurting humanity. His Kingdom offer for us to participate in bringing His purpose to fulfillment is the treasure that was hidden in the field, prior to creation. It is the Pearl for which we must be willing to trade all[51], in order for us not to become paralyzed by the past or overly enamored by the future!

Restoring God's Fatherhood is defined by Paul as "His being restored to be everything to everyone, supreme, the indwelling and controlling factor of Life."[52] This is something for which we should be willing to die. If I could give the entire world a gift, it would be to give them their Father back. That, I believe, was Jesus' own Job description. It now has become ours!

---

51 Matthew 13:44-46
52 1 Corinthians 15:28

Appendix I

I have come to believe that in these two passages that most often when Paul was speaking of the conflict of the flesh and the spirit he is referring to the human spirit and not the Holy Spirit. I believe that Paul saw the regenerated and enlivened human spirit taking ascendency in my being, causing me to become a truly spiritual person.

Romans 8:3-14

3 For what the Law could not do, weak as it was through the flesh, God did: sending His own Son in the likeness of sinful flesh and as an offering for sin, He condemned sin in the flesh,

4 so that the requirement of the Law might be fulfilled in us, who do not walk according to the flesh but according to the [human] spirit.

5 For those who are according to the flesh set their minds ["set . . . minds" does not here refer to our thoughts but to our intentions and inclinations] on the things of the flesh, but those who are according to the [human] spirit, the things of the [human] spirit.

6 For the mind set on the flesh is death, but the mind set on the [human] spirit is life and peace,

7 because the mind set on the flesh is hostile toward God; for it does not subject itself to the law of God, for it is not even able to do so,

8 and those who are in the flesh cannot please God.

9 However, you are not in the flesh but in the [human] spirit, if indeed the Spirit of God dwells in you. But if anyone does not have the Spirit of Christ, he does not belong to Him.

10 If Christ is in you, though the body is dead because of sin, yet the spirit is alive because of righteousness.

11 But if the Spirit of Him who raised Jesus from the dead dwells in you, He who raised Christ Jesus from the dead will also give life to your mortal bodies through His Spirit who dwells in you.

12 So then, brethren, we are under obligation, not to the flesh, to live according to the flesh—

13 for if you are living according to the flesh, you must die; but if by the [human] spirit you are putting to death the deeds of the body, you will live.

14 For all who are being led by the Spirit of God, these are sons of God.

Galatians 5:16-26

16 But I say, walk by the [human] spirit, and you will not carry out the desire of the flesh.

17 For the flesh sets its desire against the [human] spirit, and the [human] spirit against the flesh; for these are in opposition to one another, so that you may not do the things that you please.

18 But if you are led by the [human] spirit, you are not under the Law.

19 Now the deeds of the flesh are evident, which

are: immorality, impurity, sensuality,

20 idolatry, sorcery, enmities, strife, jealousy, outbursts of anger, disputes, dissensions, factions,

21 envying, drunkenness, carousing, and things like these, of which I forewarn you, just as I have forewarned you, that those who practice such things will not inherit the kingdom of God.

22 But the fruit of the [human] spirit is love, joy, peace, patience, kindness, goodness, faithfulness,

23 gentleness, self-control; against such things there is no law.

24 Now those who belong to Christ Jesus have crucified the flesh with its passions and desires.

25 If we live by the Spirit, let us also walk by the [human] spirit.

LIFECHANGERS ®

P.O. Box 3709 ❖ Cookeville, TN 38502
931.520.3730 ❖ lc@lifechangers.org

www.ingramcontent.com/pod-product-compliance
Lightning Source LLC
Chambersburg PA
CBHW071742020426
42331CB00008B/2134